WORKING LIVES

Photographs of workers
and their work in Scotland
1897 - 1997

BY IAN MacDOUGALL

Foreword by Campbell Christie
General Secretary, Scottish Trades Union Congress

HAMILTON

SCOTTISH LIBRARY ASSOCIATION

1997

ACKNOWLEDGEMENTS

Aberdeen City Council Library Services

East Dunbartonshire Council Library Service

East Renfrewshire Council Library Service

Edinburgh City Council Library Service

Fife Council Central Area Library Services

Fife Council East Area Library Services

Fife Council West Area Library Services

City of Glasgow Council Libraries and Archives

Highland Council Library Service

Midlothian Council Library Service

Perth & Kinross Libraries and Archive Services

Scottish Life Archive, National Museums of Scotland

Smith Art Gallery and Museum, Stirling

Stirling Council Library Service

West Dunbartonshire Library Services

West Lothian Council Library Services

Every effort has been made to seek the permission of copyright holders to reproduce photographs used in this publication.

Scottish Library Association
Scottish Centre for Information
& Library Services,
1 John Street,
Hamilton ML3 7EU

© Scottish Library Association 1997

ISBN 0 900649 97 6

Designed by GSB · Edinburgh
Cover photography:
Chris Christenson · Midlothian

Printed by BPC-AUP · Aberdeen Ltd.

The solidarity, resourcefulness, diversity and imagination which characterise trade union organisation spring directly from the experience which people gain in their working lives.

So, this *Working Lives* publication with its wonderful illustrations and explanatory text by Ian MacDougall is particularly welcome, appearing, as it does, in the Centenary year of the Scottish Trades Union Congress.

The jobs that people do, the working conditions they experience, and the patterns of ownership and employment which prevail in their industry all influence their trade union organisation - from the structure of their trade union branches, to the way they design their banners, to the way they articulate their demands, to the kind of leaders who emerge from their ranks.

The Scottish miners, to take just one example, endured particularly hard and dangerous working conditions in which each miner's safety was entirely dependent on his fellow workers.

The miners' solidarity, formed underground, shaped their trade union and community organisations and left an indelible impression, not just on the trade union movement and the STUC, but on the social, political, cultural and sporting map of Scotland.

Miners at Prestongrange Colliery, East Lothian, c.1905-14, with the manager, John Halliday, in bowler hat. Boys went down the pit at age 14.

Similar processes were in operation, of course, in many other trades and industries, and they are splendidly illustrated in this publication.

Photographs have a power which words can only rarely match and the photographs reproduced in *Working Lives* will kindle memories for many older readers and fire the imagination of a younger generation.

Everyone at the STUC, in our Centenary year, is particularly pleased to be associated with the Scottish Library Association. We share a common commitment to a well-resourced, accessible public library system.

The trade union movement's working relationship with Ian MacDougall stretches back over many fruitful years. His contribution to Scottish labour and trade union history has few equals.

I am pleased to welcome and commend this *Working Lives* publication to a wide readership in the STUC's Centenary year.

Campbell Christie, General Secretary, Scottish Trades Union Congress

Ploughmen at work with their pairs of horses in Perthshire, c.1930.
(Courtesy of Star Photos, Perth)

217155

The working lives of people in Scotland during the past eventful century is the theme of this pictorial book. It is a contribution by the Scottish Library Association toward marking the centenary in 1997 of the Scottish Trades Union Congress. The Scottish TUC has played during these past hundred years (and seems certain to continue doing so in the new century) a leading role in tackling relevant issues confronting working people throughout Scotland and in seeking to achieve their hopes and aspirations.

Above: A woman and three men stack hay at Dall, Ardeonaig, Perthshire, c.1930s.

Left: Farm workers harvesting at High Mains, Dumbarton, c.1910.

Above: Tattie howkers, including children, at Newton in Fife, c.1937.

Left: Milkmaids at Garthamlock Farm on the eastern outskirts of Glasgow, c.1910.

Right: Combine harvester at Clochton, Angus, c.1960. Mechanisation has greatly reduced the numbers of farm workers in 20th century Scotland.

The working lives this publication is concerned to illustrate are those of the great mass of the people of Scotland, those who in order to live have had to sell their labour power. This book is not concerned with that small minority composed of wealthy landowners, industrialists and investors whose huge social, economic and political power during these past hundred years has been expressed in the formula 7:84 - those 7 per cent who own 84 per cent of the wealth of Scotland.

Above: Farm workers threshing the grain harvest at Balgraystone Farm, Newton Mearns, c.1900.

Above: Women farm workers (two wearing the distinctive hats of bondagers) at Hilltown Farm, Newton, Midlothian, c.1900.

Left: Skye crofters, a decade before the foundation in 1897 of the Scottish Trades Union Congress. The men dig with the caschrom (foot plough), the women spread seaweed as fertiliser. The STUC was partly an outcome of the struggles of the Highland crofters.

Left: Landraiding crofters at Knoydart, Inverness-shire, reading court interdicts against them, November 1948. The land raid itself was defeated, but it raised again the issue of landlordism and land use in the Highlands. (Courtesy of The Herald).

The working lives of people in Scotland, as elsewhere in the United kingdom and other countries, have been subjected in the past century to flows, sometimes eddies, sometimes floods, of change. These changes have varied from the sudden, the swift, the extensive, to the moderate, the gradual, the slow, even almost imperceptible, and the limited. Two world wars, and many lesser ones, revolutions (above all the Russian Revolution of 1917) or reactions (especially the rise of Fascism and Nazism between the Wars), colonial struggles, issues such as ownership of the means of production, distribution and exchange, policies of governments national and local, equal rights for women and for ethnic or other minorities, and always the course of economic and industrial development, booms and slumps, as well as strikes and lock-outs, unemployment, short-time working, intimidation or victimisation at work, health and safety, housing - all these and many other issues, international, national and local have affected to one extent or another during the past century the working lives of people throughout Scotland.

Salmon fishers on the river Forth in Stirlingshire, c.1900.

A fishwife with her creel rests from her sales at Lasswade Brae, Midlothian.

Right: Granton, Edinburgh, trawlermen's catch is unloaded, 1958.

Opposite page: Fishermen at Anstruther Harbour, Fife, between the wars.

Fish curers on Stronsay, Orkney, 1935.

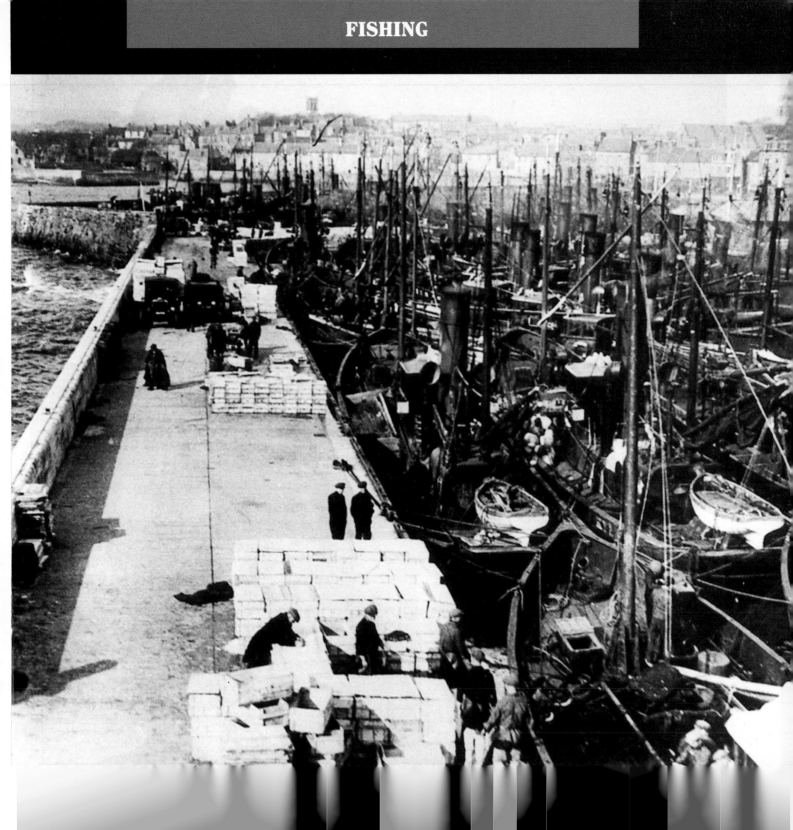

Above: Miners at Auchenreoch colliery, Stirlingshire, prepare a pit pony for descent underground c.1910-20.

Right: Miners underground at the Lady pit (Whitrigg), Whitburn, West Lothian, 1950s.

FR top: William Wishart, winding engineman at Gartshore No. 3 colliery, Dunbartonshire, c.1959.

FR bottom: Richard McGregor checking miners' lamps at Polkemmet colliery, West Lothian in the 1950s.

FUEL & POWER

Sunday work. Road transport workers, and particularly the horse-driving carters, generally worked between fourteen and sixteen or more hours a day, amounting to between 84 and as many as 100 hours a week – and no payment for overtime. Throughout the nineteenth century the traditional goal had been the three eights - eight hours' work, eight hours' sleep, and eight hours' leisure time. The miners after years of struggle won that eight-hours day or 48 hours week by the Coal Mines (Eight Hours) Act of 1908. Immediately

Above left: Workers at Granton Gas Works, Edinburgh, c.1903.
Above: Electricity generating workers, St Andrews, c.1912.
Left: Tunnellers at the Loch Sloy hydro-electricity scheme, Dunbartonshire, complete the breakthrough at Butterbridge Tunnel, December 1949.

Above: Thousands of men and women have been employed at Dounreay nuclear plant in Caithness since it was built in the 1950s.
Left: Launch of the oil-rig Penrod 64 from Marathon yard, Clydebank, September 1973.

after the Great War of 1914-18 widespread and militant demands for shorter hours were voiced through their trade union organisations and the Scottish TUC by working people in Scotland. One of the aims of these demands was to avoid the unemployment arising from demobilisation of millions of men by the armed forces and from the ending of war production. A spearhead of this shorter hours movement was the 40-hours strike in January 1919, centred on Clydeside,

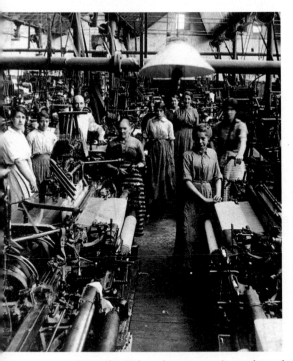

Top right: Girls and women reeding in front of a dressing machine in a Dundee jute mill, about 1900.

Above: Workers in James Slimon & Co's cotton mill at Kirkintilloch c.1910.

Right: Women workers at Strathclyde Hosiery Mill, Hardgate, near Clydebank, c.1914.

but which spread through other parts of Scotland and was supported by the Scottish TUC. The strike failed to win the 40-hour week but contributed to reductions in working hours for many workers. Further reductions followed after the Second World War, with the establishment of a five-day working week and hours generally ranging from about 40 to 45 a week. Demands for further reductions in working hours have often been made by working people through their trade unions in

Left: Women hosiery workers in Livingstone's West Lothian Hosiery factory, Bathgate, c.1920.

Women working seaming machines at Hawick Hosiery Factory, 1947.

A carpet factory worker at Bonnyrigg, Midlothian, c.1960s

Women inspecting Harris Tweed at Newall's Mill, Stornoway, 1961.

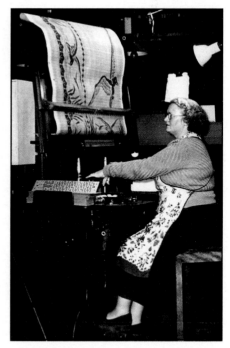

Mrs Widridge, forewoman, operatiing a piano card cutter at St Leonard's linen factory, Dunfermline, 1950s. (Courtesy of Morris Allan Collection)

the past half century, with varying degrees of success. For long it was believed that the gain of technological change would be to create opportunities for more leisure and personal development. Instead, in more recent years, some have found their hours increased not reduced, because of economic recession, mass unemployment, privatisation, the weakening of trade unionism, or other factors.

Left: Tailors working at Penicuik Co-operative Society, 1898.

Below: Women clothing workers in a new factory at Campbeltown, 1957.

Above: Women workers busy at sewing machines at J E Clarke Ltd, nightwear manufacturers in Dumbarton, 1966. (Courtesy of Frank Melvin)

Right: Women laundry workers in the Vindanda Laundry, Kirkintilloch, 1920s.

Above left: Distillery workers at Tambowie Distillery, near Milngavie, c.1900.

Above: About 1,000 fruit pickers were employed each summer at Essendy, Perthshire, when this photograph of women cooks was taken in 1912 in one of the kitchens in the pickers' shanty town there. (Courtesy of D.W.M. Davidson Collection)

Left: Bannockburn Co-operative Society grocery cart driver, c.1936.

Holidays for working people in Scotland have had a similar history during the past century. Most working people had no annual paid holidays until after (in some cases long after) the 1914-18 War – and even then were granted only two or three days a year. Since the Second World War, first a full week's paid holiday, later two weeks', and in more recent times three or more, have become more general. The number of paid public holidays – until the First or even Second World Wars generally only New Year's Day was granted, often unpaid – has also increased in more recent times to several a year. On the other hand, recent research has indicated that 11 per cent of all workers in Scotland today still do not enjoy any entitlement to holidays.

Top left: Shop workers at Lipton's cold meat counter, Barnton Street, Stirling, c.1936.

Top: Bottle labelling by women workers at Dumbarton Distillery, 1958.

Above: Washing milk bottles at Dunfermline Co-operative creamery, c.1960. (Courtesy of Morris Allan Collection)

Above left: Women and men workers at Hall's of Broxburn, West Lothian, c.1960.

Few reductions in working hours or increases in paid holidays this past century have been won without persistent struggle on the part of working people, their trade unions and the Scottish TUC.

Wages, as a result of similar pressures and agitations, also generally improved in real terms from the 1890s to the 1980s. But again there is the danger of this trend being reversed. While few are so miserably underpaid as were so many working men and women a century or less ago, research by the Scottish Low

Above: Quarry worker near Kilsyth.

Left: Inside an Aberdeen granite works.

Above: Two of some 5,000 Forestry Commission workers in Scotland in the late 1940s.

Top left: Sawmillers at Broadcroft Sawmill, Kirkintilloch, early this century.

Top right: Joiners at Callander, c.1900.

Pay Unit indicates that 42 per cent of all workers are today on low pay (especially in such occupations as hotels and catering) and some 22 per cent are below the minimum wage threshold of £4.26 per hour. A retired Penicuik farm worker has recently recalled how in 1922 aged 14 he began work on a local farm, working six days a week for 65 hours a week, for a wage of 50 pence (ten shillings) a week; seven years later, aged 21, he was working the same hours six days a week – still for 50 pence a week. The struggle by working people throughout Scotland to improve their standard of living by

Above: Painters and decorators at Stirling, 1909.

Left: Cabinetmakers at George Gray & Sons, Kirkcaldy, 1912.

winning better wages, or to defend that standard by resisting reductions, has been a constant feature of their working lives these past hundred years. Sometimes that struggle has been successful, sometimes not – but it is certain to continue.

Working conditions have generally greatly improved during the past century and more attention has been given, particularly since the Second World War and the passage of the 1974 Health and Safety at Work Act, to the question of health and safety at work. Some industries or occupations, such as mining, fishing, building, extraction of North Sea oil, and others, are by their nature dangerous. But hazards to

Top: Ferro-concrete workers, 1920s, at Girling's works, Inchterf, Stirlingshire.
Above: Building workers constructing Blackburn houses at Dumbarton, c.1955.

health and safety at work lurk to one extent or another for virtually all working people. In the past century many have lost their lives, limbs or health through industrial accidents or bad working conditions. Speaking during a debate on factory inspection at the Scottish TUC annual congress in 1962 (two years after 19 firemen had been killed at a fire at the Cheapside whisky bond in Glasgow when the walls of the building suddenly blew out), Mr Enoch Humphries, delegate of the Fire Brigades Union, said that firemen "could give many illustrations of receiving calls to factories throughout the length and breadth of the country where, because of failure to comply

Top right: Workers busy repairing boilers and tenders at Cowlairs railway engineering works, Glasgow, c.1900-10.

Above: Workers pour out of the huge Singer factory, Cydebank, c.1905.

1. Workers at Singer's, Clydebank, made over 2,500.000 screws each week early this century.

2. Sewing machine assembly line workers at Singer's, c.1964..

3. Women workers at Ferranti engineering works, Dalkeith. c.1960s. (Courtesy Campbell Harper Studios Ltd)

4. Engineers at Albion Motor Works, Glasgow, c.1950's. (Courtesy of Mrs Chalmers, Bearsden)

Foundry workers at North British Steel Foundry, Bathgate,

1.

2.

3.

4.

Top: George Cooper, Bishopbriggs, working on a turning lathe at St Rollox railway engineering workshops, Glasgow, 1986.

1. Brass Foundry workers at Normand & Thomson, Dunfermline, c.1925.

2. Workers building the aluminium factory at Fort William in the mid-1920s lived in this base camp.

3. Moulders at South Bank Ironworks, Kirkintilloch, 1980.

4. Steel products being loaded at Gartcosh Works, Lanarkshire, 1986.

with the Factories Acts, small hole-in-the-corner factories were, in essence, death traps, with staff working under conditions designed to permit employers to earn the maximum amount of profit in the shortest possible time with no question of ensuring safety from fire." Almost seven years later, in November 1968, 22 workers died in a fire behind the barred windows of the upholstery warehouse where they worked in James Watt Street, Glasgow. From the deaths of six miners caused by an inrush of water at Devon Furnacebank No.1 pit in Clackmannanshire on the day that the Scottish TUC was founded in 1897, through such stark statistics, for example, that in 1919 one in every fifteen railway shunters was injured and one in every 425 killed at work, to the Piper Alpha disaster in 1988 when 167 North Sea oil workers lost their lives, working men and women have been subject to death and injury in their employments.

Above: Packers in the warehouse at Kali Iron Works, Lennoxtown, c.1950.
Below: Foundry workers in the erecting shop, Douglas & Grant, Kirkcaldy, 1903.
Below right: Kit Sked, Cousland village blacksmith, Midlothian, c.1980s.

Right: Finishing shop workers at the Lion Foundry, Kirkintilloch, c.1930s. The foundry was closed in 1984.
Opposite page: After a two-year lay-off shipyard workers at John Brown & Co Ltd, Clydebank, resume work, 4 May 1934, on the liner Queen Mary.

SHIPBUILDING

Platers' shed at Beardmore's shipyard, Dalmuir, c.1904-06.

Drawing office workers at Beardmore's shipyard engine shop, Dalmuir, c.1906-07.

Unemployment and short-time working have been among other burdens suffered by many working men and women in Scotland as elsewhere during the past century and still are so at present. Falling demand for products or services, mechanisation or computerisation, the decline or working out of resources such as coal or fish, the import of cheap foreign goods, the impact of wars, lack of investment, government policies - these and many other factors, varying in time and place, have cost the jobs of masses of working men and women in Scotland. Whole industries, such as coal-mining, shipbuilding, paper-

Top: These women worked as polishers at the building of the liner Queen Mary at Clydebank, 1934.

Above: Riveters at work in a Glasgow shipyard (probably Yarrow's), 1950.

Left: Shipyard workers building the liner Queen Mary at Clydebank, 1934.

making, have been decimated or have disappeared, traditional skills superseded by machines or computers, and the lives of working people and their families badly affected.

To try to defend and improve their conditions of work and their wages, as well as other aspects of their lives, working men and women have long formed or joined trade unions. Unions existed for nearly two centuries in Scotland before the Scottish TUC was founded in 1897. Some unions have been purely Scottish, others United Kingdom wide; some confined to skilled workers who had

Above: Drillers at work in a Glasgow shipyard (probably Yarrow's), c.1950.

Left: A riveter at work at John Brown & Co Ltd's shipyard, Clydebank. (Courtesy of The Herald)

Top: Printers at P & D Lyle, Dalkeith, c.1910.

Above: Women workers at Kinleith paper mills, near Edinburgh, c.1900.

Women workers predominate in the finishing house at Ellangowan paper mill, Milngavie, 1948.

Above: The machine house at Ellangowan paper mill, Milngavie, 1948.
Below: A linotype operator setting up the Lennox Herald, 1958.

served formal apprenticeships in their trade, others general unions enrolling mainly the unskilled (in the sense of not having served any formal apprenticeship), or industrial unions with members only or predominantly in a single industry (such as coal-mining or railways), or unions for women only (while some others in the earlier half or so of the past century excluded women from membership) — in short, a great variety of union organisation, with varying influence, numbers of members, length of

Top: Ann Magee, aged 16, youngest employee of William Collins & Sons, publishers, Bishopbriggs, 1977.

Above: About 900 workers were employed at the huge Corpach pulp and paper mills, Inverness-shire, from opening in the 1960s till closure in 1980.

Above: A young carter with his horse, Kirkcaldy High Street, 1890s.

Right: Tramway crews' farewell: the last tram runs from Glasgow to Dalmuir West, 6 September 1962.

Below: Railway men at Balloch, c.1900. (Courtesy of B. Jardine)

Tramcar driver Charles McKinlay and conductress in Dumbarton, 1914. (Courtesy of Charles McKinlay)

Above: Engine driver Willie Stanners of St Rollox, Glasgow, driving his steam engine Merlin in Perthshire in 1963-4 - the last days of steam.

Above right: Constructing Great Western Road boulevard, near Duntocher, 1920s.

existence, and success. In some occupations such as hotels and catering, shops (other than Co-operative Society stores) and office work (other than Civil Service or local government), it has always proved difficult to achieve effective union organisation; and indeed only for a short period in the 1970s has a majority of the working population in Scotland been organised in trade unions. But trade unions have played a constant, and sometimes a crucial, part during the past century in the lives of many working people in Scotland.

Driver W. Forrest with his bus at Kirkintilloch, 1936.

Without trade-union organisation and action in that period wages and conditions would have been worse. As the banner of the Aberdeen sawmillers' union proclaimed about the time the Scottish TUC was formed in 1897:

"Combination is strength,
And we Sawmillers know it.
And we're here with our emblems
And Mottoes to show it.
Wake up, brother toilers.
Stand fast for the right.
Our strength lies in Union —
Unite! Then Unite!!"

Below left: These lorry drivers take a break at Rest and Be Thankful, Arrochar, Argyll, 1930s.

Below: Edinburgh Corporation bus workers with their buses, 1958.

Air transport provided increasing employment in Scotland as the 20th century progressed. This plane is landing on the Cockle Shore, Barra, in the Outer Hebrides, on its daily flight from Renfrew, 1948.

Above: Dunfermline District roadmen at Crossgates, Fife, 1911.

Above right: A lollipop man on duty at Dowanhill Primary School, Glasgow, c.1950.

Right: St Andrews fire brigade, 1920s.

Far right: Firemen of Milngavie, c.1940s.

Below left: P.C. Henry Mackenzie at Bonnyrigg-Lasswade, c.1900.

Below right: A group of Glasgow police, c.1906.

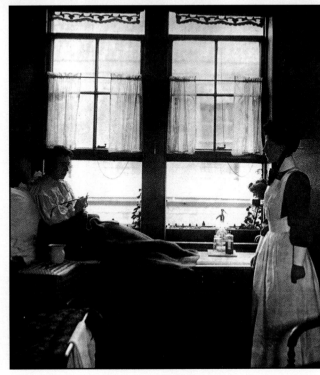

Trade union activities this past century that have affected the working lives of men and women in Scotland have ranged from the quiet routine of representations to or negotiations with employers, to dramatic action such as strikes or resistance to employers' lock-outs of their workers. The great national miners' strikes or lock-outs in 1912, 1920, 1921, 1926, 1972, 1974, and 1984-5 are some examples among innumerable others of the vast range and recurrence of such struggles (one peak in which was the great nine days General Strike in 1926) that in many industries or occupations and localities in Scotland have affected working men and women and their families to one extent or another at one time or another. On the other hand, many

Top left: Librarians of Perth and Kinross County Library load up a mobile library for its service to readers throughout the county, 1968. (Courtesy of Perthshire Advertiser)

Top: A teacher with his class at Clydebank School, c.1914.

Above: School dinner ladies at Douglas Academy, Milngavie, c.1970s.

Left: A nurse tends a consumptive woman patient at the Royal Victoria Hospital, Edinburgh, c.1905.

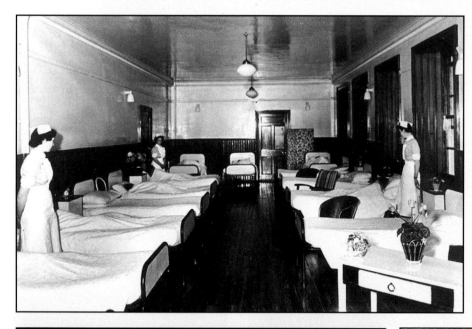

working people this past century were never themselves on strike or locked-out.

The working lives of women during the past 100 years have undergone significant changes. Economic, social and political developments, pressure by women activists, legislation against sex discrimination, and many other factors have advanced the position of women in employment. Yet that advance has been uneven and incomplete. For example, pay of women in full-time employment in 1994 was on average only about 72 per cent of that of men; in secondary schools in Scotland

Top: Nurses with their patients in Bangour Village Hospital, West Lothian, c.1957.
Above: Some of the nurses of Edinburgh Royal Infirmary. c.1927.
Right: Margaret Cairns, "the island's nurse" on Fair Isle, c.1960s/70s.

Typists in the office of Kali Nail Works, Lennoxtown, c.1940s/50s.

Women stokers at Singer's factory, Clydebank, in the 1914-18 War.

Women steel workers, Methil, Fife, in the 1914-18 War.

Munitions work at Anderson's Garage, Newton Mearns, during the Second World War: these workers are making gun parts.

The experiences of working men and women in Scotland during the past century have therefore been extremely varied. Many have been fortunate to find real satisfaction in their work, in some cases despite poor wages or unhealthy or unsafe working conditions. Even when work itself might be boring or burdensome or both there has very often been the companionship and friendship of fellow workers to relish. As an elderly woman who for many years worked as one of a permanent squad of women and girls in the potato and other fields of south-east Scotland for a particularly mean employer has recently put it: "Ah loved gaun oot tae the tatties and if ah was able now ah wid still go oot. It wis the company. Ye had good company, every one o' them wis good company."

Top: Tenement in Glasgow Road, Dumbarton, bombed by Hitler's air force, 1941. Working people suffered severely in the Clydeside blitz then.

Left: Women munitions workers at Barry, Ostlere & Shepherd, Kirkcaldy, in the 1939-45 War.

Right: March of men and women from Alexandria to Dumbarton, c.1930, to demand increased rates of relief from the County Council. (Courtesy of James Russell and Mary Drain)

Below: The Hungry 'Thirties: a long queue of unemployed men at Clydebank Labour Exchange, 1932.

That immense variety of experience in the working lives of men and women this past century cannot, of course, be comprehensively presented in a work of this nature. But the photographs here, it is hoped, offer at least two signposts. One is to that variety of experience, employment, industry, locality, and period, and to the skills and patience, courage and endurance, and sheer smeddum of so many so-called "ordinary" working people. The other signpost is to the photographic collections in public libraries throughout Scotland, collections that deserve to be more widely known and used.

Harry McShane (centre, with cap) and John McGovern (right) lead Hunger Marchers from Glasgow to London in 1934.

Most of the photographs here have been provided by public libraries in Scotland. Supplementary illustrations, particularly of some more recent aspects, have come from the Scottish Life Archive of the National Museums of Scotland. Every effort was made to contact copyright holders, but in some cases without success. Warm thanks are therefore due to all those librarians and archivists who have contributed these photographs, and to other copyright holders for their permission. Particular thanks are due to Alan Reid, Don Martin and Robert Craig of the Scottish Library Association for their energy and commitment in building and smoothing so many paths toward publication.

Ian MacDougall, February 1997.

Top: Band of the Singer's workers on strike, March 1911, outside Kilbowie Station.

Right: Clydebank engineering and shipbuilding workers take part in the 1957 national strike.

Soup kitchen run by strikers at United Turkey Red Company, Alexandria, 1931. (Courtesy of Mrs Mary Drain)

Countless children of school age in Scotland have delivered milk, newspapers or rolls during the past century. Here children deliver milk in pitchers at Aboyne, c.1916.

Milk boys in Candle Close, Leith, 1953.

Top: Clay pipemakers, Leith, 1904.

Centre: Coopers at work at Broxburn between the Wars.

Bottom: Roslin gunpowder mill workers at a works council election in 1929.

FALKIRK COUNCIL
LIBRARY SUPPORT
FOR SCHOOLS

Right: Housewives in Partick, Glasgow, c.1950.

Below: Women workers making novelty products at Lillyburn Works, Milton of Campsie, c.1981.

Left: Agnes Stewart (right), first forewoman to be appointed in the Singer Factory, Clydebank, 1963. (Courtesy of Singer Co.Ltd.)

An engraver at work at Edinburgh Crystal Glass Company, Penicuik.